Hidden in My Heart

Memorizing Scripture to Fight the Fight of Faith

Truth:78

Production:
Designer: Shannon Brown
Editorial Review: Karen Hieb

Hidden in My Heart: Memorizing Scripture to Fight the Fight of Faith

Edited by Sally Michael and Candice Watters

Published in the United States of America by Truth78.

ISBN: 978-1-952783-45-6

Truth:78

Equipping the Next Generations to Know, Honor, and Treasure God

Truth78.org
info@Truth78.org
(877) 400-1414
FighterVerses.com

Dedication

To the faithful Christians through the centuries who have hidden God's Word in their hearts, that they might not sin against God (Psalm 119:11).

May God add many to their number.

Acknowledgments

There have been many people who have helped with Fighter Verses since its inception in a third-grade classroom in the mid-'70s, through its debut as a church-wide memory program at Bethlehem Baptist Church of Minneapolis, Minnesota 25 years ago, and on into today.

Though many people contributed in countless ways over the years to the development and growth of the Fighter Verses, a special thanks is due to Linda McIntire, David Michael, Brian Eaton, Randy and Kathi Westlund, Betty Dodge, John Piper, and Char Ransom.

To those unmentioned—the countless friends and partners in ministry who have contributed to and memorized the Fighter Verses over the past four decades—thank you!

Contents

Blessed is the man who walks not in the counsel of the wicked, nor stands in the way of sinners, nor sits in the seat of scoffers; but his delight is in the law of the LORD, and on his law he meditates day and night. He is like a tree planted by streams of water that yields its fruit in its season, and its leaf does not wither. In all that he does, he prospers. (Psalm 1:1-3)

Finally, be strong in the Lord and in the strength of his might. Put on the whole armor of God, that you may be able to stand against the schemes of the devil. For we do not wrestle against flesh and blood, but against the rulers, against the authorities, against the cosmic powers over this present darkness, against the spiritual forces of evil in the heavenly places. (Ephesians 6:10-12)

Foreword

By Brian Eaton

I grew up in Southern Minnesota on a family farm. My dad, 97, harvested his last crop in 2015, after more than 68 years of farming. He and my mom, 94, celebrated their 75th wedding anniversary last year. They moved off the farm after the last crop, but I will always have excellent memories of the farm.

One of those memories recurred every year as my extended family traveled to the farm for Christmas. The day included many traditions, but I'll mention just two. We would arrive to a huge Christmas meal that my mom had prepared. Afterwards we would all participate in a Christmas program, from the Word, with many Christmas songs and a few skits. The program concluded with a time of sharing, giving everyone a chance to share what the Lord had been doing in our lives the past year.

A number of years ago, my dad, with tears welling up in his eyes, began to tell us of some events that took place the week before. He had attended a farming presentation in Minneapolis, which is about an hour and a half from the farm. He planned to watch a movie after the presentation. Yet, for some reason, when the presentation ended, my dad didn't feel like going to the movies and started for home.

My mom also had plans that day. She attended a church event in the afternoon and then returned home. While walking to the house, she lost her balance and fell into a snowbank. She could not get up.

When my dad arrived home, he found my mom still lying in the snow. She had been there nearly two hours. My dad was emotionally distraught because he wasn't physically strong enough to help her up. With tears in his eyes, he went back to his car to phone for help. He cried out to the Lord, "I'm going to need some of Your help here!" When he returned, inexplicably, he was able to lift my mom up and get her into the house.

There wasn't a dry eye in our family as my dad recounted this traumatic experience. We were pained for Mom and yet rejoicing at the goodness of God to answer Dad's prayer.

It was no coincidence that our church was memorizing Isaiah 46:3-4 that week with Fighter Verses:

> *"Listen to me, O house of Jacob, all the remnant of the house of Israel, who have been borne by me from before your birth, carried from the womb; even to your old age I am he, and to gray hairs I will carry you. I have made, and I will bear; I will carry and will save."*

Truly God was faithful. He had carried my mom from birth to every one of her gray hairs. He had indeed saved her—from the snowbank, but most importantly, for eternity.

God not only strengthened Dad to lift Mom out of the snow. He also strengthened my faith as I thought about her fall and rescue in light of the Isaiah passage. Without that truth, I would have been tempted to think God was unloving to allow my elderly mom to lie in the snowbank for two hours. I would have missed the greatness and wonder of God. I would not have been positioned to proclaim God's goodness. Because I was memorizing Isaiah 46:3-4, I could say with assurance, and by experience, "He will carry the gray and elderly, He will bear them up through His strength. Even when my dear dad was unable—look what He did for Mom! Praise God, He will carry, He will save."

I am grateful to the Lord for Sally Michael. Hers is a life saturated with the Word. She speaks, prays, and counsels the Word *from memory*. I am also thankful for the Fighter Verses program that Sally helped to launch over 25 years ago to equip the saints to fight the good fight of faith. Because I have been memorizing Fighter Verses over the years, the Lord has brought His Word to mind giving me the opportunity to think and act biblically, like when my mom fell in the snow. God's Word kept me from focusing on her distress and led me to rejoice in His care for her.

May this book kindle your desire to build up such a reserve of Scripture. Let the stories and tools gathered here inspire and equip you to begin or keep on going. And may the Lord lead and sustain you in this essential spiritual discipline.

Preface

The day started out wonderfully. We got an early start on our trip from Minneapolis to Chicago. My husband David and I (Sally) were looking forward to attending a conference, and our two daughters, Amy and Kristi, were excited about spending a few days with their cousins. The atmosphere in our 1982 Pontiac Bonneville station wagon was jubilant—until we heard a clunking sound. The car shuddered and the engine sputtered as we slowly made our way off the highway exit and came to a standstill. There were furrowed brows and lots of anxious questions. The atmosphere was tense. After examining the engine, David said what threatened to squelch any remaining remnant of the once-jubilant mood, "I think we threw a rod. I'll have to walk to find help." (This was in the days before cell phones.)

"Threw a rod" did not sound like a simple fix. In fact, it sounded serious. David started walking to find help while the two girls and I stayed in the car shivering as the car cooled down to match the single-digit Wisconsin temperature. It slowly sank in that Chicago was a lost dream and we would not be getting there any time soon. One daughter started crying. The other was visibly upset. All their plans were spoiled.

How does a mom or dad redeem a situation like this?

Our Bibles were packed away in our suitcases, but we had been memorizing Scripture since the girls were in preschool. Now at elementary school age, the girls had an arsenal of "Fighter Verses" that could preach to their souls. So I asked them, "Do you know a Fighter Verse that could help us in this situation?"

One of them dolefully sighed, "I suppose Romans 8:28. 'All things work together for good.'" This was a fitting verse, but they had not yet caught its reality. "Are there other verses you can think of?" I asked.

One by one they started reciting verses, and little by little their mood changed. Granted, they weren't jubilant, but they grew expectant. After quoting about 25 verses, one of the girls blurted out, "I wonder what God is going to do in this situation?" In a matter of minutes, I had watched the Word of God transform their hearts from anxious frustration to hopeful expectation.

What did God do? Well, we had the car towed to a garage, the girls got to spend a few hours in a local public library reading some favorite books, and people from our church attending the same conference stopped and picked us up with enough room in the van for all four of us. But best of all, our family witnessed God's faithfulness, wisdom, and goodness. His Word is powerful and heart-transforming.

Why did our daughters' perspectives change? Because Scripture was a ready and true witness to our souls. We didn't have our Bibles in our hands—they were still packed in our suitcases. This happened because we had verses in our hearts.

I am very much aware that Scripture memorization has largely fallen by the wayside in our day...But let me say as graciously but firmly as I can: We cannot effectively pursue holiness without the Word of God stored up in our minds where it can be used by the Holy Spirit to transform us...I know it requires work and is sometimes discouraging when we can't recall accurately a verse we have worked hard to memorize. The truth is, however, all forms of discipline require work and are often discouraging. But the person who perseveres in any discipline, despite the hard work and discouraging times, reaps the reward that the discipline is intended to produce."

—Jerry Bridges[1]

1. Jerry Bridges, *The Discipline of Grace: God's Role and Our Role in the Pursuit of Holiness.* (Colorado Springs, Colo.: NavPress, 1994), 175.

Chapter 1
Reviving Scripture Memory

"Scripture memorization has largely fallen by the wayside in our day..."

—Jerry Bridges

Some things *should* go by the wayside—things like '70s platform shoes and jumpsuits for men; Victorian jewelry, pictures, and art made from human hair; and creamed tuna and peas on toast. (Surely we're not alone on that last one.)

Though some fading trends are a welcome relief, the waning of Scripture memory is a tragic loss. Sadly, the decline Jerry Bridges observed in 1994 is even more pronounced today. What has your experience been? Does your church encourage Scripture memory for children *and* adults? Do your Christian friends work at memorizing verses and encourage you to join them? Is Scripture memory a regular practice in your home?

If you can answer *yes* to these questions, thank God for your community. You are in a rare place. Still, the question remains: are we untroubled that a discipline that helps us pursue holiness is so rarely encouraged, supported, or given a place of prominence in the church? Yes, some things *are* worth leaving behind, but memorizing God's Word is not one of them.

A Perspective on How We Got Here

Memorizing Bible verses encourages our faith, helps us fight sinful desires, deepens our understanding of God and His Word, informs our prayers, and fuels our witness to unbelievers. How is it possible that such a helpful habit—an essential spiritual discipline—is largely missing in our churches and homes?

A quick look at education trends offers some clues. Generations ago, memorization was an integral part of teaching. Children regularly memorized poetry and math tables by reciting them aloud. The presidents of the United States, state capitals, the periodic table, and famous speeches were committed to memory. That all changed around the time people were wearing bell bottoms. Schools moved away from rote memory work to group projects and perceptions-based instruction. Then computers, the internet, and smartphones made memorizing nearly obsolete. Regrettably, the church has followed the same trend. Why memorize a verse when you can just "google it"?

In the past 50 years, our schools have traded memorization for "higher" forms of learning such as critical thinking and problem-solving. While these are important skills, without first filling minds with vital information, there's nothing to think critically about. A person's mind must feed on ideas before he can draw conclusions and form convictions. In our day, information is coming at us from all sides, but there is little encouragement to linger over the ideas it contains. How much less are we encouraged to think deeply, unhurriedly about God's Word—to consider its truthfulness, meaning, and significance, or to discern how it applies to daily life?

Memorization Makes Meditation Possible

> The failure to linger is the reason why many fail to remember or find their hearts warmed by the fire of God's Word. —Donald Whitney[2]

Professor of Biblical Spirituality at Southern Seminary, Donald Whitney laments the neglect of Bible memory for what it costs a Christian's heart. He echoes the psalmist in Psalm 1:1-3,

> *Blessed is the man who walks not in the counsel of the wicked, nor stands in the way of sinners, nor sits in the seat of scoffers; but his delight is in the law of the LORD, and on his law he meditates day and night. He is like a tree planted by streams of water that yields*

2. Donald S. Whitney, *Spiritual Disciplines for the Christian Life.* (Colorado Springs, Colo.: NavPress, 1991, 2014), 49.

its fruit in its season, and its leaf does not wither. In all that he does, he prospers.

Do you want to be blessed by the Lord? To live a fruitful and godly life? To know God intimately and walk in sweet communion with Him throughout your day? Psalm 1 tells us how to do that: meditate on God's Word, day and night.

The Hebrew word translated *meditate* means to speak or mutter. To meditate on God's Word means to speak it to yourself throughout the day. The way to do this is not by simply passing the words of the Bible through your mind briefly as you read it, but by memorizing Scripture. Memorization makes meditation possible. A memorized verse can hum in the back of your mind all day. When your thoughts wander, the memorized Word is there as a familiar route to follow, bringing your thoughts back to fruitful paths. The more you consider a verse, rolling it over in your thoughts, the deeper its meaning goes, not only into your mind, but also by God's grace, into your heart. This is how God encourages our hearts, informs our decisions, strengthens our convictions, and deepens our relationship with our heavenly Father. The memorized Word speaks to a Christian's soul as his mind recalls it. The Holy Spirit uses the Word to shape how believers think and how they live.

Without meditation, we have "minds like sieves," says author Lou Priolo. He explains the importance of Scripture meditation in his book, *Teach Them Diligently,* where he paraphrases Puritan preacher Oliver Heywood:

> Lack of meditation is the primary reason that so many professing Christians, in spite of exposure to the most excellent teaching, still remain ignorant, unstable, and unfruitful, "ever learning, but never able to come to the knowledge of the truth." Instruction flows in upon them from all sides; but their hearts and minds are like sieves, out of which everything runs as fast as it is poured in. The impressions which truth makes on their minds are as temporary as characters traced on the sands of the seashore, which the next wave erases forever. But meditation imprints truth deeply on the conscience, and engraves it on the tablets of the inner man, as with the point of a diamond or laser beam. It thus becomes incorporated into the soul; and forms, as it were, a part of it; and

> it is ever present, to regulate the heart's affections and to control and guide all of its movements.[3]

Priolo goes on to add his own thoughts to Heywood's:

> Meditation fastens into our hearts truths which we received but have not yet assimilated into our character. Meditation is a means the Spirit of God effectively uses to permanently amalgamate into our character that truth which previously we may have only received intellectually or superficially—truth that had not yet been digested and become a part of our makeup.[4]

The Holy Spirit does not work in a vacuum. He works through the divinely inspired Word. When you memorize God's Word, you can practice the sort of day and night meditation David extols in Psalm 1. Meditation leads to insights you would otherwise miss. The Holy Spirit is faithful to bring situations into our lives to show us the truthfulness and wisdom of God's Word. As we ponder Scripture, it becomes the beliefs and convictions we internalize and the measure by which we discern other ideas and philosophies we encounter. Most importantly, as you meditate on God's Word and accept it by faith, you meet God.

A Soldier in the Fight

> *I have thought it necessary to send to you Epaphroditus my brother and fellow worker and fellow soldier, and your messenger and minister to my need, (Philippians 2:25)*

Paul describes Epaphroditus as his brother, fellow worker, and fellow soldier. *Brother* and *fellow worker* make sense. As believers in Jesus, Paul and Epaphroditus were children of God (John 1:12) and therefore, the two were brothers. Their shared partnership in advancing the gospel made Epaphroditus a fellow worker with Paul. But *fellow soldier*? Why did Paul call him that?

Elsewhere he tells us they were "engaged in the same conflict" (Philippians 1:30), fighting not "against flesh and blood, but against the rulers, against the authorities, against the cosmic powers over this present darkness, against the spiritual forces of evil in the heavenly places" (Ephesians 6:12), and "keep[ing] alert with all perseverance"

---

3. Lou Priolo, *Teach Them Diligently: How to Use the Scriptures in Child Training.* (Stanley, N.C.: Timeless Texts, Inc., 2000), 86-87.
4. Ibid.

(6:18). They put on "the whole armor of God" in order that they might "be able to stand against the schemes of the devil" (6:11). They were true soldiers, working out their salvation "with fear and trembling" (Philippians 2:12). Their battles were spiritual.

Those who believe in and receive Jesus as Savior are, along with Epaphroditus, brothers and sisters in the family of God. We are fellow workers in God's Kingdom, spreading His glory and the message of salvation from generation to generation to the ends of the earth. We are also fellow soldiers, fighting the fight of faith as we also work out our "own salvation with fear and trembling" (Philippians 2:12).

Paul wrote to the new Christians in Colossae about the need for perseverance. Like them, Christians today must engage in the ongoing battle of "continu[ing] in the faith, stable and steadfast, not shifting from the hope of the gospel" (Colossians 1:23). Every Christian must speak truth to his soul, fighting not only the temptations of the flesh, but also battling *for* faith. The assaults of the enemy come in the form of lies that threaten to diminish the joy of our salvation and love for the gospel, undermine our belief in the promises of God, numb our hunger for God, distract us from single-minded devotion to Christ, and dull our appetites for spiritual things. The Bible helps us defeat those lies.

Whitney describes the centrality of God's Word to fighting the battle. in *Spiritual Disciplines for the Christian Life*:

> The Word of God is the "sword of the Spirit," but the Holy Spirit cannot give you a weapon you have not stored in the armory of your mind. Imagine yourself in the midst of a decision and needing guidance, or struggling with a difficult temptation and needing victory. The Holy Spirit rushes to your mental arsenal, flings open the door, but all He finds is a John 3:16, a Genesis 1:1, and a Great Commission. Those are great swords, but they're not made for every battle.[5]

More than 20 years ago, I (Sally) faced an unexpected battle. I had prayed that I would truly understand how to abide in Christ—day by day, hour by hour, moment by moment. I also prayed that I would be sanctified in a number of areas. Not long after, I experienced some physical problems that led to insomnia. At its height the insomnia was

5. Donald S. Whitney, *Spiritual Disciplines for the Christian Life*. (Colorado Springs, Colo.: NavPress, 1991, 2014), 42.

so severe that I would only get about two hours of sleep every four nights. It was a struggle to think. I had to read my Bible with my finger under each word as I fought to concentrate on what I was reading. I would read and reread a passage trying to clearly get it in my head.

What kept me going during that long, excruciating year? The hundreds of verses I had memorized. I would repeat them over and over throughout the day—sometimes repeating a verse 25 or 30 times.

> *Weeping may tarry for the night, but joy comes with the morning... Many are the afflictions of the righteous, but the LORD delivers him out of them all...This light momentary affliction is preparing for us an eternal weight of glory beyond all comparison, as we look not to the things that are seen but to the things that are unseen. For the things that are seen are transient, but the things that are unseen are eternal...Count it all joy, my brothers, when you meet trials of various kinds, for you know that the testing of your faith produces steadfastness.*[6]

When reading my Bible was difficult, these verses, and many others I had memorized, gave me a firm foundation for trusting God in the midst of suffering. God's Word *is* powerful! We cripple our faith when we do not have it solidly fixed in our minds to cling to when we need it most.

Fit and Ready Words

> *A word fitly spoken is like apples of gold in a setting of silver. (Proverbs 25:11)*

Who hasn't struggled at times to know the right words to counsel someone, encourage a discouraged friend, witness to an unbeliever, or pray for someone in need? Often our words fall short of being helpful, hanging lifeless over the conversation. In sharp contrast, God's Word "is living and active, sharper than any two-edged sword," says the writer to the Hebrews, "piercing to the division of soul and of spirit, of joints and of marrow, and discerning the thoughts and intentions of the heart" (Hebrews 4:12).

That sword is alive with God's power. Countless times I've had friends pour out their concerns to me, and I've been clueless about what to

6. Psalm 30:5b; Psalm 34:19; 2 Corinthians 4:17-18; James 1:2

say. In such moments, I pray and ask God for a Word. I run through my mental list of memorized verses until God leads me to just the right one. They have been a comfort, a gentle rebuke, a source of hope, or a confirming word at just the right time. Those verses are the words of the Wonderful Counselor.

There are no words more comforting than those soaked in God's Word. There are no prayers uttered that lead us into the presence of God like Bible-saturated prayers. There is no speech that can touch the human heart like Scripture-filled speech. There are no assertions that bring more clarity or wise counsel than Bible-infused guidance. There are no soul-converting words apart from the two-edged sword of the Word of God. In situations when such words are called for, we can't go flipping through our Bibles to find a fitting verse. We must have them stored in our heart so the Holy Spirit can bring them to mind. He jogs our memory to say what He knows each person needs to hear. If there are no verses to draw from, if we are ill-prepared, how many opportunities to be a help and comfort to others will be lost?

John Piper tells of the time, early in his pastorate, when he felt his lack of the memorized Word:

> My first or second year of pastoring I was called to the hospital—quickly. I went without my Bible. [Church member] Rollin Erickson's wife just had a heart attack. I walked into a room of probably 20 family members that didn't know if she was alive or dead—as she is in surgery. Rollin gave me a big hug and said, "John, give us a Word from the Lord." Now, if I had my Bible I would have opened it to a Psalm or something. I didn't have my Bible, and for whatever reason at age 35 my mind went blank.
>
> I felt so humiliated. It was horrible. Here are 20 people, and the husband of a dying woman says, "Give us a Word from the Lord." I can't even remember what I said. I probably said, "Let's pray," and tried to paraphrase some Scripture. I went home and got on my knees that afternoon. I said, "Lord Jesus, that will never happen again." I opened to Psalm 46—"God is our refuge and strength." I have been able to quote Psalm 46 verbatim for the last 28 years. I decided that Psalm 46 is going to be in my head because it is so useful all the time.[7]

7. John Piper, "How Do You Avoid Forgetting Scripture That You've Memorized?" July 17, 2010, desiringgod.org/interviews/how-do-you-avoid-forgetting-scripture-that-youve-memorized

God used that experience to light a fire in John Piper's soul to memorize Scripture. May He grant you that same fire.

"...for my soul, for the warfare of my life, and for ministry in hospitals and counseling sessions, I want a cluster of texts at my disposal. Decide what those are, put them on a piece of paper, and review them until you have them down...really nail down a cluster of soul strengthening words."[8] —John Piper

Memorize for Worship and Prayer

Meditating on verses we have memorized can lead us to greater depths of worship of Almighty God. Psalm 103 reveals the beauty of God's character and provides a host of reasons to praise Him. Just reading this psalm should fill the believer's heart with praise. Meditating on it can bring forth even more praise. Reciting psalms like this after memorizing them elicits praise from the mouth of believers to their Heavenly Father.

> *Bless the LORD, O my soul, and all that is within me, bless his holy name!*
>
> *Bless the LORD, O my soul, and forget not all his benefits,*
>
> *who forgives all your iniquity, who heals all your diseases,*
>
> *who redeems your life from the pit, who crowns you with steadfast love and mercy,*
>
> *who satisfies you with good so that your youth is renewed like the eagle's.*
>
> *The LORD works righteousness and justice for all who are oppressed.*
>
> *He made known his ways to Moses, his acts to the people of Israel.*
>
> *The LORD is merciful and gracious, slow to anger and abounding in steadfast love.*
>
> *He will not always chide, nor will he keep his anger forever.*

8. John Piper, "How Do You Avoid Forgetting Scripture That You've Memorized?" July 17, 2010, desiringgod.org/interviews/how-do-you-avoid-forgetting-scripture-that-youve-memorized

He does not deal with us according to our sins, nor repay us according to our iniquities.

For as high as the heavens are above the earth, so great is his steadfast love toward those who fear him;

as far as the east is from the west, so far does he remove our transgressions from us.

As a father shows compassion to his children, so the LORD shows compassion to those who fear him.

For he knows our frame; he remembers that we are dust.

As for man, his days are like grass; he flourishes like a flower of the field;

for the wind passes over it, and it is gone, and its place knows it no more.

But the steadfast love of the LORD is from everlasting to everlasting on those who fear him, and his righteousness to children's children,

to those who keep his covenant and remember to do his commandments.

The LORD has established his throne in the heavens, and his kingdom rules over all.

Bless the LORD, O you his angels, you mighty ones who do his word, obeying the voice of his word!

Bless the LORD, all his hosts, his ministers, who do his will!

Bless the LORD, all his works, in all places of his dominion. Bless the LORD, O my soul!

The memorized Word also provides Christians with language for prayer. How often do you hear prayers that sound like repetitive phrases requiring little thought—"Dear God, bless our day. Bless the missionaries. Keep them safe." Children, especially, tend to pray this way—"Dear God, thank You for the nice day. Help me to have a good birthday party. Bless my soccer tryouts." There is nothing wrong with these and similar prayers if they're spoken from a sincere heart. But memorizing Scripture provides us with meaty prayers, guiding our heart in praying God's words for His purposes. Those are the prayers Jesus promised God would answer (John 15:7).

I once sat in on a sixth-grade Sunday school class where the worship leader ended with a song about God's goodness. He then asked the children to pray by starting their prayers with the words, "God, You are so good because..." I was astounded by what I heard from the class:

> "God, You are so good because while we were yet sinners, Christ died for us."
>
> "God, You are so good because You work all things for good for those who love You, who are called according to Your purpose."
>
> "God, You are so good because You did not spare Your own Son but sent Him to die for us."

The students prayed for several minutes, offering prayer after prayer—most containing ideas from memorized verses. What a different experience it was from the anemic prayers I had heard before we started memorizing verses in our church. The children were praying thoughtful prayers, prayers infused with the words of Scripture, prayers expressing true declarations of God's goodness.

When Scripture informs our prayers, we are praying God's own thoughts back to Him, bending our will to His glorious purposes.

Memorize for a Changed Heart

How often do we read the Word, set it aside, and go about our day without thinking how what we just read applies to life—how the truth should inform our words, actions, and thoughts; how God's Word should shape our hearts? It's easy to run the words through our minds, but so much harder to have them sink into our hearts. We can read the Bible and walk away unchanged.

The Apostle James understood this when he wrote:

> *But be doers of the word, and not hearers only, deceiving yourselves. For if anyone is a hearer of the word and not a doer, he is like a man who looks intently at his natural face in a mirror. For he looks at himself and goes away and at once forgets what he was like. But the one who looks into the perfect law, the law of liberty, and perseveres, being no hearer who forgets but a doer who acts, he will be blessed in his doing. (James 1:22-25)*

> in a way that pleased God, and to fight against my own wisdom of commanding "make me joyful."[10]

Acting on the truth of God's Word transformed a very sick man, banished his despair, informed his mind with truth, and caused him to worship God. By "being no hearer who forgets but a doer who acts," (James 1:25), he was blessed in his doing. In order to "do" the Word, we have to know the Word. As we memorize it, we can practice it in our daily lives, pleasing the Lord by walking in His ways, and honoring Him by worshiping Him.

Infinitely Worth the Effort

> Pray for strength as you begin [memorizing Scripture], and let the Bible talk to you powerfully, and commit to do it. It [is] just infinitely worth it.—John Piper[11]

The resolve to memorize Scripture is a work of God. You may be motivated to start memorizing Bible verses in your own strength, but only God can provide the will and deep conviction necessary to sustain a lifelong habit of Bible memory. It is a discipline, one that provides great spiritual benefit. But as with other spiritual disciplines, you will encounter spiritual opposition. The enemy of our souls hates well-armed saints. Rest assured that "he who is in you is greater than he who is in the world," the evil one who "prowls around like a roaring lion, seeking someone to devour."[12] Seek the Lord and His favor as you begin to memorize; and as you continue memorizing, seek the Lord.

Don't be discouraged if, at first, it is difficult to memorize and retain verses. The ability to memorize improves with practice. The more we exercise our brains, the easier memorization becomes. In order to remember newly memorized verses, it is necessary to repeat them often. The key to retaining verses over time is, as John Piper says, "Review, review, review...Average folks like me have to work real hard to memorize the first time, and then recurrently review to keep it."[13] At first it is time consuming, but eventually, a verse becomes cemented in your mind and you will be able to review it very quickly.

---

10. Brian Eaton. "The Power of the Word: The Memorized Word: A Power for Salvation, Satisfaction and Sanctification." Children Desiring God (Truth78) 2016 National Conference. Indianapolis, Indiana.
11. John Piper. "Practical Tips for Bible Memory," *Ask Pastor John*, January 7, 2014, desiringgod.org/interviews/practical-tips-for-bible-memory
12. 1 John 4:4; 1 Peter 5:8
13. John Piper, "How Do You Avoid Forgetting Scripture That You've Memorized?" July 17, 2010, desiringgod.org/interviews/how-do-you-avoid-forgetting-scripture-that-youve-memorized

Although you will not always have perfect recall, you will likely remember portions of verses: "His mercies are new every morning; find rest, O my soul, in God alone; never will I leave you… " These fragments of truth will inform your soul and give you much to meditate on. And there will be many verses you do recall quickly and accurately—certainly many more than if you had never attempted to memorize at all. Let Jerry Bridges's words encourage you to persevere:

> I know it requires work and is sometimes discouraging when we can't recall accurately a verse we have worked hard to memorize. The truth is, however, all forms of discipline require work and are often discouraging. But the person who perseveres in any discipline, despite the hard work and discouraging times, reaps the reward that the discipline is intended to produce.[14]

What are those rewards? John Piper, my former pastor, who encouraged his congregation to memorize the Fighter Verses together, summed up the benefits this way:

1. …I just got an email last week from a man who said he took up the challenge and memorized Ephesians and just was able to say it for the first time all the way through as he was jogging.
2. The focus on children and church-wide memorizing has awakened old people who had given up and now many are working at it again.
3. The effect on prayer meetings (I attend five 30-minute prayer meetings each week besides staff and elder prayer times) is rich: we hear each other praying the verses, not just saying them.
4. The whole point is to learn to fight the fight of faith (1 Timothy 6:12) with the Word of God and this too is growing as people come to understand that specific verses provide specific daggers to defeat the lies of the evil one hour by hour.
5. Who can know or measure the mighty invisible effects of the Word on the souls of our people![15]

---

14. Jerry Bridges, *The Discipline of Grace: God's Role and Our Role in the Pursuit of Holiness.* (Colorado Springs, Colo.: NavPress, 1994), 175.
15. John Piper, email message to Kathi Westlund, April 6, 2005.

Maybe someday you, or your pastor, will similarly describe the rewards of memorizing Scripture. If you ask God for the desire and will to hide His Word in your heart, the effect on your soul—and on the people around you—will be incalculable. Consider one elderly saint and her end-of-life dependence on the memorized Word. Let her story inspire you. Ask God to give you the heart to memorize His Word for the first time. If you've already begun, ask for fresh vision to press on in the essential habit of Bible memory.

A woman in our church encouraged her husband's aunt to start memorizing Scripture when she retired. "Aunt Amy" was not highly educated...Though she only started memorizing in her 60s, she filled numerous notebooks, writing out her memory verses over and over. Eventually, she succumbed to Alzheimer's and by the time she was 80 years old, she did not recognize her nephew or his wife—her regular caregivers. She could, however, recite memory verse after memory verse. When her mind could no longer hold on to the most basic things, God's Word remained to speak to her soul. What a way to end life and enter glory![16]

Truly, memorizing God's Word *is* "infinitely worth it."

16. Adapted from Kathi Westlund. "Bible Memorization." Children Desiring God (Truth78) 2011 Conference. truth78.org/training?training=873&product_list_limit=all

Chapter 2
Stand on His Promises

"I tell thee, friend, there are some promises that the Lord hath helped me to lay hold of Jesus Christ through and by, that I would not have out of the Bible for as much gold and silver as can lie between York and London piled up to the stars."[17]

—John Bunyan

Puritan John Bunyan spent 12 years in prison for refusing to stop preaching God's Word. It was there that Bunyan penned his most influential work, *The Pilgrim's Progress.*

In a biographical sketch of Bunyan, John Piper shows the link between Bunyan's dependence on God's promises in prison and the plight of Christian, Bunyan's well-known main character. In the story, Christian and his companion, Hopeful, find themselves imprisoned, deprived of food and water, beaten, and despairing of life itself:

> ...on Saturday about midnight the prisoners began to pray; and they continued in prayer until almost the break of day. Now a short while before it was daylight, Christian, like someone suddenly amazed, broke out with a most passionate exclamation. "What a fool I have been, to lie like this in a stinking dungeon, when I could have just as well walked free. In my chest pocket I have a key called Promise that will, I am thoroughly persuaded, open any lock in Doubting-Castle."

17. John Piper, "His Wounded Heart Bled Bible: John Bunyan (1628-1688)," August 31, 2019, desiringgod.org/articles/his-wounded-heart-bled-bible

> "Then," said Hopeful, "that is good news. My good brother, do immediately take it out of your chest pocket and try it."
>
> Then Christian took the key from his chest and began to try the lock of the dungeon door; and as he turned the key, the bolt unlocked and the door flew open with ease, so that Christian and Hopeful immediately came out.[18]

Like Christian, knowing and believing God's promises are also our "key of Promise." This is an essential reason to memorize Scripture. May we earnestly seek to respond in faith and obedience to Paul's charge:

> *Therefore take up the whole armor of God, that you may be able to withstand in the evil day, and having done all, to stand firm. (Ephesians 6:13)*

Memorize in Calm to Prepare for Storms

Had Christian and Hopeful not known God's promises by heart, they would surely have died of despair. We also face times when it's impractical, or even impossible, to grab a Bible or mobile device to look up a relevant promise from Scripture.

Sarah House, a stay-at-home mom and blogger, recounts how taking time to memorize Scripture in a calm season of life benefited her soul when a family emergency hit in a chaotic season of life:

> In the midst of running errands, I received a text from my mom. My cousin had a serious infection. He was fading fast. When we arrived at the hospital, he was confused and anxious. As I held his hand and wondered if this was goodbye, I spoke the first verse that came to mind:
>
> > *"Fear not, for I have redeemed you; I have called you by name, you are mine. When you pass through the waters, I will be with you; and through the rivers, they shall not overwhelm you; when you walk through fire you shall not be burned, and the flame shall not consume you. For I am the LORD your God, the Holy One of Israel, your Savior." (Isaiah 43:1b-3a)*
>
> When I memorized that verse as a teenager, our family was not in a moment of crisis. It was just the next verse on the list. However,

18. John Bunyan, *The Pilgrim's Progress*, 1678, p. 132. desiringgod.org/books/the-pilgrims-progress

> in that hospital room, I was thankful for that strong, memorized Word to cling to.
>
> When the moment of trouble arrives, we rarely have time to search through our concordance for the perfect verse to quench the fiery darts flying at us. May I challenge us to consider how we are fortifying our souls for the days of trouble? After all, we have been promised that trouble will come (John 16:33).

House concludes,

> Don't wait for the hospital room to find that verse you need... Prepare. Prepare your heart for the next family gathering, for the "random" moment you run into an old friend who has just heard bad news, or even for the next time your child has a nightmare. Jesus said troubles would come—and He did not leave us without help...
>
>> *Let the word of Christ dwell in you richly, teaching and admonishing one another in all wisdom, singing psalms and hymns and spiritual songs, with thankfulness in your hearts to God. And whatever you do, in word or deed, do everything in the name of the Lord Jesus, giving thanks to God the Father through him. (Colossians 3:16-17)*[19]

When the Word of Christ dwells in us, it can helpfully flow from us in every season of life.

Bleeding Bible

Trapped in a dark dungeon, Christian had only his memory to recall the verses that unlocked his prison. Piper notes the significance of where Bunyan located Christian's key:

> Three times Bunyan says that the key was in Christian's *bosom,* or chest. I take this to mean that Christian had hidden it in his heart by memorization and that it was now accessible in prison (though he had no Bible available) for precisely this reason. This is how the word sustained and strengthened Bunyan....Everything he wrote was saturated with the Bible.[20]

---

19. Sarah House, "Memorize the Word in Calm, to Prepare for Life's Storms," December 10, 2019, truth78.org/blog/post/memorize-the-word-in-calm-to-prepare-for-lifes-storms
20. John Piper, "His Wounded Heart Bled Bible: John Bunyan (1628-1688)," August 31, 2019, desiringgod.org/articles/his-wounded-heart-bled-bible

A quick look at modern copies of Bunyan's works reveals hundreds of Scripture references listed in the footnotes. His stories are brimming with Bible. Bunyan said of his works, "...my Bible and Concordance are my only library in my writings."

"Read anything of his," said Charles Spurgeon,

> and you will see that it is almost like reading the Bible itself. He had read it till his very soul was saturated with Scripture; and, though his writings are charmingly full of poetry, yet he cannot give us his *Pilgrim's Progress*—that sweetest of all prose poems—without continually making us feel and say, "Why, this man is a living Bible!"[21]

Spurgeon said, "Prick him anywhere—his blood is Bibline, the very essence of the Bible flows from him. He cannot speak without quoting a text, for his very soul is full of the Word of God." Though we may not know the definition of the antiquated *bibline,* the meaning is clear: "He bled Bible."[22]

Pilgrim's Progress has never been out of print since its release in 1678. Some might call Bunyan a publishing superstar. But to him that would be worthless acclaim. The wealth he sought was knowing God's Word by heart, being strengthened by God's promises, and persevering through God's Word amidst intense suffering. When everything in his life was shaking, God's Word hidden in his heart was solid rock under his feet.

---

21. John Piper, "His Wounded Heart Bled Bible: John Bunyan (1628-1688)," August 31, 2019, desiringgod.org/articles/his-wounded-heart-bled-bible
22. Ibid.

Chapter 3
When Memorizing is Hard

"While still a child, hymn writer Fanny Crosby committed to memory the first four books of the Old Testament, the four Gospels, the book of Proverbs, many of the Psalms and many favorite individual chapters."[23]

—Henry Gariepy

When John Piper introduced church-wide Bible memory at Bethlehem Baptist Church of Minneapolis, Minnesota in 1997, he challenged the congregation's assumption that Scripture memory would be too hard:

> If I offered you $1,000 for every verse you memorized in the next week, how many do you think you could memorize? Yet God says of his word in Psalm 19:10–11, "They are more desirable than gold, yes, than much fine gold; sweeter also than honey and the drippings of the honeycomb. Moreover, by them thy servant is warned; in keeping them there is great reward." The real value of the word is far greater than $1,000 a verse. The question is this: Do you believe it?[24]

"I Can't Memorize."

For all it's benefits, it can feel like memorizing is too hard, or something that should only be required of grammar school children. If you think "I can't memorize," take heart. "Don't say you can't memorize because you have a bad memory," says Jon Bloom. "That's *why* you need to

23 Henry Gariepy, *Songs in the Night.* (Grand Rapids, Mich.: Eerdmans Publishing Co., 1996), 129.
24 John Piper, "Thy Word I Have Treasured in My Heart," January 5, 1997, desiringgod.org/messages/thy-word-i-have-treasured-in-my-heart

memorize."[25] His article, "Ten Reasons to Memorize Big Chunks of the Bible" debunks a host of excuses.

It's simply not true that we can't memorize. What we see and think about and practice regularly, we remember. Most of us have more things memorized than we even realize: baseball stats, football scores, friends' and family members' birthdays, recipes, song lyrics, phone numbers (in pre-smartphone days), and more. You likely have ad jingles stuck in your head that you wish you could forget. Everyone has the God-given ability to recall things they have memorized.

What comes naturally to mind for you? Lines from movies? Song lyrics? Sports stats? The same mental process that made those things stick works for Bible memorization, too, whether you're young or old. Like chicken marinating in vinaigrette, our minds will have the flavor of what they're soaked in. We tend to memorize things we look at all the time and things that are important to us.

"I'll Just Google It."

One of the most common objections to memorizing Scripture is that we think the Internet makes it unnecessary. If we can look up any verse with just a quick key-word search on a device we always have with us, why bother memorizing? Bloom says that's exactly why we *should* memorize:

> Unfortunately, the Internet is teaching us how not to read. We are becoming information scanners, quickly browsing but not digesting very much. We are losing patience for deeper, more reflective reading. Memorizing longer passages of Scripture forces us to reflect deeply on meaning and application.[26]

"I'm Too Busy to Memorize."

The best advice for how to memorize also answers another common objection: *I don't have enough time.* But we all have time—24 hours every day. It's not a matter of quantity, but priorities. How are you spending the time you've been given? When something is important to us, we say we can "make time for it." Obviously we can't actually

25. Jon Bloom, "Ten Reasons to Memorize Big Chunks of the Bible," May 16, 2014, desiringgod.org/articles/ten-reasons-to-memorize-big-chunks-of-the-bible
26. Ibid.

make time, but we do get to decide how we'll spend it. When we make Scripture memory a priority, we are more inclined to set aside time to memorize. The way to do that is to plan for regular reflection and review.

We not only have the same number of hours to get things done, we also have pockets of time that, if used intentionally, can lead to great strides in memorizing verses. Rather than flipping on the radio or streaming music or a podcast when running errands or commuting to work, why not put that time to use reviewing your memory verses.

Singer/songwriter Jimmy Needham says he reviews his verses in the shower:

> I line the wall with print-outs of the passages I've learned in gallon zip lock bags. It's unconventional, but it works for me. Maybe in your struggle to memorize the Bible you have not yet [persisted] to the point of mounting zip lock bags. What creative approach might work for you and your schedule?[27]

One friend keeps 3x5 cards with his current memory verses attached to the visor of his car with a rubber band so he can review them while waiting at stoplights and easily remove them to use while standing in line when he gets to where he is going. We can memorize while brushing our teeth, walking on the treadmill, folding laundry, washing dishes. The options are many. Printing verses on cards and posting them around the house—on the fridge, over the sink, on bedroom and bathroom mirrors—can prompt us to use spare moments to work on our verses.

Practice may not make anything perfect on this side of heaven, but it does make us more proficient. As with physical exercise, Scripture memory gets easier the more we do it. Even if it's slow going at first, the benefit of having God's Word stored in our heart is worth every effort (Psalm 119:11).

The more often a person reads, repeats, and reviews verses, the more quickly and firmly he'll have passages memorized. When Christians make the effort to remember verses by memory, asking God to help them as they go, it's remarkable what can happen.

27. Jimmy Needham, "Advice for Better Bible Memory," April 23, 2016, desiringgod.org/articles/advice-for-better-bible-memory

Chapter 4
Practical Tools for Memorizing

"How do you memorize Scripture? First of all, by praying for discipline and setting aside time."[28]

—John Piper, *Ask Pastor John*

Asking God for help and making a plan for Bible memory sounds basic enough, but they're essential first steps. Left to ourselves, even the best intentions to memorize wane. We need supernatural help to grasp the meaning of the words we're working at remembering. Paul said, "The natural person does not accept the things of the Spirit of God, for they are folly to him, and he is not able to understand them because they are spiritually discerned" (1 Corinthians 2:14).

Once God gives us the desire to memorize, we still need to block off time to do it. Where can time to memorize be found? King David sought God in the night when he was upon his bed (Psalm 63:6) and early in the morning (Psalm 119:147). Job rose early to pray (Job 1:5). Whether morning or night, Jesus went off by Himself "to desolate places [to] pray" (Luke 5:16). Most English translations say He did this *often*. If Jesus needed time alone to listen to His Father's words, how much more do we! God's Word is our very life (Deuteronomy 32:47).

Setting aside and protecting time to memorize is essential and can make the difference between good intentions and the transformation that comes from being immersed in God's Word. Thankfully, it doesn't take long hours to memorize. What's key is a routine, a "settled pattern"

28. John Piper, "How Do You Memorize Scripture," *Ask Pastor John*, August 31, 2006, desiringgod.org/interviews/how-do-you-memorize-scripture

of Scripture memory, says Andrew Davis, author of *An Approach to Extended Memorization of Scripture.*

A Little Over a Long Time

Read and repeat for a short time every day. That's the simple approach Davis recommends. He has successfully used this method to memorize not only verses, or even chapters, but whole books of the Bible.

"Saying a verse one hundred times in one day is not as helpful as saying it every day for one hundred days," says Davis. "The absolute key to successful Scripture memorization is repetition over a long time period."[29]

"If you repeat a verse by memory once a day for 100 days, it will be in your permanent long-term memory," writes Jon Bloom.[30] Verses can be easily memorized and retained with an investment of only about 10 to 15 minutes each week. If you invest a few more minutes, you can retain hundreds of previously memorized verses. A sample schedule looks like this:

Sunday

Read the week's passage to be memorized with surrounding verses so you can see it in its context. Ask the Lord to help you commit the passage to memory, apply it to your life, and use it to bless others.

Monday

Read the passage with the reference 10 times aloud. Then cover the passage and say it aloud with the reference 10 more times, looking if necessary. Say each memorized passage from previous weeks one time aloud with references.

"Each time you say it, emphasize a different word," suggests John Piper, using Romans 8:1 as an example:

> There *is* therefore now no condemnation for those who are in Christ. There is *therefore* now no condemnation for those who are in Christ. There is therefore *now* no condemnation for those

29. Andrew Davis, *An Approach to Extended Memorization of Scripture*, (Durham, N.C.: FBC Durham), 15. scripturememory.com/products-resources/resources/free-downloads#
30. Jon Bloom, "Ten Reasons to Memorize Big Chunks of the Bible," May 16, 2014, desiringgod.org/articles/ten-reasons-to-memorize-big-chunks-of-the-bible

who are in Christ. There is therefore now *no* condemnation for those who are in Christ.[31]

Tuesday

Cover the passage of the week and try to say the verse aloud with its reference 10 times, looking if necessary. Say each memorized passage from previous weeks one time aloud with references.

Wednesday-Saturday

Recite this week's passage and each memorized passage from previous weeks one time aloud with references.

Pray, Repeat, Review

Ask the Lord to help you retain what you memorize and use it to minister to others and feed your own soul. Repeat memorized passages once daily for at least 50 days. They're more likely to move into long-term memory when you do. After that, it's helpful to review them once every week or two.

More Ways to Memorize

Repeating a verse out loud is a proven way to memorize. But it's not the only way. Sarah House offers four different strategies aimed at hiding God's Word in our hearts: read the Word, meditate on the Word, study the Word, and sing the Word.

Read the Word

House points to the blessed man of Psalm 1, who makes the Word of God his constant study:

> *[H]is delight is in the law of the Lord, and on his law he meditates day and night. He is like a tree planted by streams of water that yields its fruit in its season, and its leaf does not wither.* (Psalm 1:2b-3a)

She says,

> Drink from the Word. Do it daily. Do it when you need it most. In those hectic, harried days of infants and toddlers, I needed

31 John Piper, "Practical Tips for Bible Memory." January 17, 2014, desiringgod.org/interviews/practical-tips-for-bible-memory

the Word at night to bring peace and rest. Now that the kids are older, the Word is my morning wakeup, giving me hope and focus for the day ahead...Sometimes I read chapters, sometimes just a single chapter. The point is to read it, know it, pray through it, and submit to it. There is not a burden we carry or a trouble we face that cannot be helped by a better knowledge of what God has spoken to us:

> *The law of the Lord is perfect, reviving the soul; the testimony of the Lord is sure, making wise the simple; the precepts of the Lord are right, rejoicing the heart; the commandment of the Lord is pure, enlightening the eyes; the fear of the Lord is clean, enduring forever; the rules of the Lord are true, and righteous altogether. More to be desired are they than gold, even much fine gold; sweeter also than honey and drippings of the honeycomb. Moreover, by them is your servant warned; in keeping them there is great reward. (Psalm 19:7-11)*[32]

Do you drink the water of the Word daily, setting aside time before the demands of the day distract you? A wise Christian once said, "meet with God before you meet with men." That's literal but figurative, too. Before we pick up a digital device with all its imposing alerts that start our minds racing, we do well to give God our first moments for Bible reading and prayer.

Meditate on the Word

We need to drink from the Word daily, but it's also good to slow down and savor it—to meditate on it rather than just rushing each day's Bible reading plan. House explains,

> It is good to read through the whole Bible, but we should not be content with just a broad overview. We must learn to "camp out" in a text. Different passages speak more poignantly to us in different seasons, and they are worth digging into. For example, as a single woman, I anchored my soul in the sovereignty of God expressed in the book of Ruth. While preparing for marriage, it was John 15. This summer it was Psalm 103...

32. Sarah House, "Memorize the Word in Calm, to Prepare for Life's Storms," December 10, 2019, truth78.org/blog/post/memorize-the-word-in-calm-to-prepare-for-lifes-storms

Take time to read deeply: look up cross references, learn the historical context, and read commentaries to see what theological gems scholars have gleaned. Does a certain passage grip your heart?...When trials come, rehearse it in your mind until your soul is refreshed in its truth.

> *My soul will be satisfied as with fat and rich food, and my mouth will praise you with joyful lips, when I remember you upon my bed, and meditate on you in the watches of the night; for you have been my help, and in the shadow of your wings I will sing for joy. My soul clings to you; your right hand upholds me. (Psalm 63:5-8)*[33]

The Lord has given us precious words of encouragement for every season and trial in life. Are you wrestling with fear? Cling to Psalm 56:3-4. Are you battling sin? Meditate on Romans 12:1-2 . Are you anxious? Rest in Philippians 4:6-8. Are you struggling with assurance of salvation? Savor the deep truths of Romans 8:29-30.

Study the Word Under Trustworthy Teachers

The Lord fills us with His Spirit to help us understand the Word. He has also called pastors and elders to give us the sense of the text so we can understand its meaning (Nehemiah 8:8). House encourages her readers to seek out faithful preaching for meditating on the Word at times when they can more easily pay attention.

> [A]s a mom with young children around me in the service, I rarely have the opportunity to listen undistracted on a Sunday morning—not to mention the Sundays we stay home with sick children. However, we live in a digital age. Many churches make their sermons available online. Find and listen to sermons by trustworthy pastors that will help you understand the Word better, as well as how to accurately apply it to your life.
>
> > *[R]eceive with meekness the implanted word, which is able to save your souls. (James 1:21b)*[34]

Has your pastor preached on a passage you are trying to memorize? That would be an ideal sermon to revisit. If he hasn't, likely other

---

33 Sarah House, "Memorize the Word in Calm, to Prepare for Life's Storms," December 10, 2019, truth78.org/blog/post/memorize-the-word-in-calm-to-prepare-for-lifes-storms
34. Ibid.

faithful ministers of the Word have. We have a wealth of sermons, books, and Bible resources we can access.

Sing the Word

What better way to hide God's glorious truths in your heart than with a song? Are you listening to music that will fill your heart with the Word? House suggests:

> Stock your music library with songs grounded in the Word that will lift your heart to God (artists like Keith & Kristyn Getty and Fernando Ortega do this well). Play them as you go about your household tasks or as you drive around in the car. Study the lyrics and think through the truths they speak. Listen to them until they penetrate your memory.
>
>> *It is good to give thanks to the Lord, to sing praises to your name, O Most High; to declare your steadfast love in the morning, and your faithfulness by night,...For you, O Lord, have made me glad by your work; at the works of your hands I sing for joy. (Psalm 92:1-2, 4)*[35]

35. Sarah House, "Memorize the Word in Calm, to Prepare for Life's Storms," December 10, 2019, truth78.org/blog/post/memorize-the-word-in-calm-to-prepare-for-lifes-storms.

Chapter 5
Memorizing with Children[36]

"My mother stored my memory, which was then very retentive, with many valuable pieces, chapters, and portions of scripture, catechisms, hymns, and poems. When the Lord at length opened my eyes I found great benefit from the recollections of them."[37]

—John Newton, former slave ship captain, Anglican minister, and author of beloved hymn, "Amazing Grace"

Why should children memorize Scripture? There are many reasons. As people made in God's image, children need to know what their Creator has said about who He is, who they are, and what He expects of them. One of the best ways to teach them these vital truths is through Scripture memory. By God's design, that's an activity well-suited to children.

Memorization Comes Naturally for Children

They memorize easily, often effortlessly. And they *will* memorize something—either the philosophy of the world or the truth of the Word. Take advantage of this God-given ability for the benefit of your child's spiritual awakening and growth. The window of opportunity is wide open for about 12 years. After that, memorizing gets more difficult. That is, unless a child has been trained already in the habit of memorization.

36. Portions of this section adapted from Kathi Westland. "Bible Memorization." Children Desiring God (Truth78) 2011 Conference. truth78.org/training?training=873&product_list_limit=all
37. Ruth Bell Graham, *Prodigals and Those Who Love Them: Words of Encouragement for Those Who Wait* (Grand Rapids, Mich.: Baker Books, 1991, 1999), 23-24.

Things Learned Early Stick for Life

What verses or poems can you recall easily? Likely they were learned in childhood. Though it is not impossible for adults to memorize, it gets harder as we age. In contrast, young children's minds aren't cluttered. Their brains are elastic and beg to be stretched. It is easy for most young children to memorize. Often they memorize entire books that have been read to them only a few times. If the habit of Bible memorization begins at a young age and is encouraged, it will become as regular in their lives as brushing their teeth or making their beds. Once it is established as part of their routine, the habit will likely last a lifetime.

Memorizing Scripture Provides Children with an Ever-Present Counselor and Protector

Parents can't always be with their children. But when the Word of God dwells in them richly, they are never alone. They have wise counsel with them at all times, counsel that is much more powerful than parents' words. They have an ever-present shield of God's Word to protect them from the inevitable attack of the enemy.

Children Have Real Struggles

Their separation anxiety, fear of the dark, fear of storms, and encounters with playground bullies are every bit as real as an adult's anxiety over work, pain in relationships, and fear of death. Children need God's Word to guard their hearts and minds just like grown-ups do.

The Memorized Word is a Means to Loving God and Obeying Him

What does your child do when someone speaks harshly to him? If he's been memorizing verses like Proverbs 15:1, "A soft answer turns away wrath, but a harsh word stirs up anger," he may be moved by the Holy Spirit to speak gently. The more children memorize, the more passages the Spirit can bring to mind as He forms their consciences and awakens them to their need for God.

When children see a biblical truth at work in a situation, and the Spirit impresses that truth on their hearts, a godly response is more likely to follow. It may take the form of fitting behavior, respectful attitudes, or even worship of God as they are awed with the truth of His Word.

The Word at Work in Young Lives

When our daughter, Kristi, was three years old, she was reminded in Sunday school that God made everything. As we left the house one day, seeing the house across the street, she said, "God made the house."

Her older sister, Amy, being six years old and possessing more knowledge of house building, corrected her, "A man made the house."

They disputed this for a bit and then I stepped in. "You are both right. A man did take a hammer and some nails and pounded some boards together to make a house. But who gave the man the tree to make the wood? And who gave the man the muscles to pound a hammer? And who gave the man a mind to know how to make a house?"

At this, little three-year-old Kristi said, "Every good and perfect gift comes from above." Then simultaneously, Amy and Kristi began singing, "God is so good, God is so good, God is so good, He's so good to me."

How did this happen? The Holy Spirit took the Word they had memorized, brought it to mind at the appropriate time, and enlivened it so that it bore fruit in the heart of two little children. —Sally Michael

Practical Guidance

Children's ability to memorize and retain Scripture is raw material. Like an uncut diamond needs a jeweler, children need parents and other adults in their lives to model and encourage memorization, and lead them in the verses they choose to memorize. Parents are the primary influence on children and the ones appointed by God to lead them in knowing and memorizing His Word (Deuteronomy 6:7; Psalm 78:5-7). Sunday school teachers can play a support role in the classroom, encouraging a lifetime of Bible memory.

Simple repetition is the best way to lead children in memorization. Speak the verse aloud for them, and then ask them to say it with you several times. Look at each word, explaining the biblical meaning of any that are unfamiliar. Taking time to understand the meaning of the words is a big help not only to memorizing, but even more importantly, to applying those words to our lives. The more you take time to learn what a verse or passage *means*, not just what the words say, the more it will equip your children and you to fight the fight of faith.

The Real-Life Game

As your children's collection of memorized verses grows, you can play games to help them review. Describe real-life situations (e.g., "Imagine you're on the way to the hospital in an ambulance...," or "that we run out of gas in a remote area...," "or that you just found out that the vacation we've been waiting for has to be cancelled..."). Then ask them what verses would help them in those situations. This helps children retain the verses they've memorized and teaches them how to apply God's Word to their lives.

Whiteboard Game

Print the whole passage and reference on a whiteboard or chalkboard. Have your child(ren) repeat it aloud several times, then start erasing one word at a time, having the child(ren) repeat the verse each time you take a word away, until the whole verse is erased. This even works with pre-readers.

Pencils, Markers, and Pens

Copying memory verses into a notebook by hand can help children retain what they're learning. Most children love to draw. Illustrating the verses they're memorizing can help them remember the verse, as well as be an encouragement to others. You can paste their illustrations into cards to send them to out-of-town grandparents or other relatives, write thank-you notes, send get-well cards to ailing friends, or write cheerful words to someone who's discouraged.

When Memorizing is Difficult

A child's response to memorizing Bible verses may be groans or resistance. Given free time, children naturally want to play with toys or friends—to do anything but memorize. If Scripture memory has not been a part of your child's experience, talk about why it's important to memorize God's Word, why it's not an optional activity, and why you're committing to working with him to learn the verses.

Once they see you embracing memory work, and as you talk about the enemy's efforts to make it hard, most children will want to join you. They enjoy the challenge of Bible memory and find it relatively easy. Some, however, do have a harder time. Simply not having such children memorize isn't a good solution, though, because every child *needs* the Word of God to be equipped to fight life's battles. If your child struggles to memorize, patiently struggle along with him.

Meditating on a verse or passage over many days, or even months, will eventually lead to memorization. Maybe not word-for-word, but the themes and truths of that passage will begin to take root in your child's heart. Be patient. Even if you think nothing is sticking, time spent with your child reading, speaking, writing, drawing, and pondering God's Word is time well spent. It will reap a harvest. God's Word always produces spiritual fruit:

> *"For as the rain and the snow come down from heaven*
> *and do not return there but water the earth,*
> *making it bring forth and sprout,*
> *giving seed to the sower and bread to the eater,*
> *so shall my word be that goes out from my mouth;*
> *it shall not return to me empty,*
> *but it shall accomplish that which I purpose,*
> *and shall succeed in the thing for which I sent it." (Isaiah 55:10-11)*

Pray for your child, and with your child, asking God to help you both remember what He has said. Every child has an avenue into his heart and mind. Sometimes it's hard to find. Pray for wisdom and ask the Spirit of God to help you. He will show you the way into your child's heart.

Every child needs God's help to memorize—God is the one who gives us the ability to know and remember anything (Psalm 94:10). So whether your children remember after just a few read-throughs, or it takes them months to be able to recall even a short passage without help, parents should encourage children to ask for God's help to store up God's Word in their hearts.

Scripture teaches us how to pray. We can pray for the desire to memorize (Psalm 119:64). We can ask God to make us, and our children, hungry for God's Word (Jeremiah 15:16). We can pray that we would be confident that God's Word is true and take refuge in it (Psalm 119:160; Proverbs 30:5).

Praying for and with your children about memorizing Scripture is one of the greatest things you can do. In Deuteronomy 6:6-7, the Lord declares,

> *And these words that I command you today shall be on your heart. You shall teach them diligently to your children, and shall talk of them when you sit in your house, and when you walk by the way, and when you lie down, and when you rise.*

If the Lord commands us to teach His Word to our children, we can know that He will hear us when we seek His help to memorize.

Godward Recognition[38]

Ultimately, love for God and His Word should be what drives us to memorize passages of the Bible. Having God's Word stored up in our minds and hearts is its own reward. Still, a few thoughtful incentives, small prizes, or milestone celebrations—like when a child has memorized 25 verses—can motivate children, and even youth, who are new to Bible memory.

How can you foster God-honoring thankfulness, not self-centered pride, when giving prizes and praise? By coupling recognition and rewards with prayerful thanksgiving and encouragement. Pray with your children, thanking God for giving them the desire and ability to memorize. You might say something like this:

> "Heavenly Father, thank You for giving Julie the ability and diligence to memorize Your Word. I pray she will hide these verses in her heart so that she might not sin against You. May she think about these words day and night. May Your words give her joy, encouragement, and hope in You. May Your words cause her to love and trust and follow Jesus every day.
>
> "And Lord, please give everyone in our family (or class) the desire, and diligence, to memorize Your Word. Help each of us to love You and Your Word more and more. May we taste and see that Your Word is sweeter than honey and brings joy to our hearts."

Praying this way points the child being recognized, as well as any others involved, to look Godward. It affirms and recognizes the child's

38. Adapted from Jill Nelson, "Godward Recognition for Bible Memory," December 7, 2016, truth78.org/blog/post/godward-recognition-for-bible-memory

diligence, while praising God as the ultimate source and power behind his ability. It also reminds siblings or classmates of the main purpose for memorizing Scripture:

How can a young man keep his way pure?
By guarding it according to your word.
With my whole heart I seek you;
let me not wander from your commandments!
I have stored up your word in my heart,
that I might not sin against you. (Psalm 119:9-11)

Chapter 6
Church-Wide Bible Memory

Let the word of Christ dwell in you richly, teaching and admonishing one another in all wisdom, singing psalms and hymns and spiritual songs, with thankfulness in your hearts to God.

—Colossians 3:16

Memorizing Scripture with other Christians is one of the best motivations to memorize. It helps those who are reluctant to try and creates momentum as the group makes progress together. The church community provides support and encouragement for growing in this key spiritual discipline.

Church-wide memory also has many benefits. When groups memorize Scripture together, the members deepen their dependence on God's Word. As they continue memorizing together, they grow in Word-centered friendships. Memorizing Scripture enriches believers' prayers for one another, helping them to pray according to God's will as it is revealed in His Word. Shared memorizing also builds unity that is essential to the body of Christ (Ephesians 4:13-16; Colossians 3:14).

There is a unique benefit, however, when church leaders make Scripture memory a priority in the life of the church, and Scripture memory becomes part of the church's DNA. Verses are uttered in prayers, read in notes, quoted to each other for encouragement, pronounced in a blessing, used to commission a missionary, and that's just the beginning. Consider Brian Eaton's testimony:

As a young boy who grew up in church and attended Sunday school, we were always given a verse to memorize. But it never felt important to me; nor did it seem that important to my Sunday school teachers.

What if it weren't that way? What if church leaders and teachers invested in church-wide Bible memory?

Ask yourself:

- What if the memorized Word was on the church's website or bulletin every week?
- What if a pastor included a portion of the memorized Word in his welcome or benediction?
- What if elders prayed the Word from memory?
- What if the worship pastor incorporated the memorized Word into the worship set?
- What if, on a regular basis, the pastor asked someone from the congregation to recite the memorized Word, and if no one in the congregation volunteered, an elder stood up to recite it?
- What if our children experienced the positive overflow of the memorized Word in the lives of their friends, parents, Sunday school teachers, elders, and pastors?
- What if our homes and churches became the place where children received encouragement to keep going with Bible memorization?
- What if the pastor dedicated one sermon a year to the priority of the memorized Word, even quoting his sermon text from memory?
- What if one Wednesday night a year the church focused on reinvigorating and inspiring the body to memorize Scripture?
- What if a church believed memorization was so important that they created a task force of members to think of new and creative ways to encourage Scripture memorization?
- What if the memorized Word was a visible priority within the church?

What would happen in your church experience, and the lives of your church family, if this list was reflected in your church? Sound ambitious, even impossible? Believe it or not, this is not hypothetical. It describes what happened at Bethlehem Baptist Church under John Piper's leadership when he and his team of leaders adopted the Fighter Verses Program.

Promoted by the senior pastor, elders, pastors, children's workers, and parents, Fighter Verses became part of the church's DNA. Everyone was encouraged to participate—young and old, single and married, male and female, leaders and lay people. Some senior saints started memorizing for the first time in their lives and found great blessing from struggling to learn the weekly verse.

They memorized, not as an intellectual exercise or to take pride in accomplishment, but as the means to live in "a manner worthy of the Lord, fully pleasing to him: bearing fruit in every good work and increasing in the knowledge of God" (Colossians 1:10). They memorized in order to know and love God more, to grow in loving others, to become faithful disciples of Jesus. The simple act of memorizing a weekly Scripture passage changed people dramatically, because Bible verses are not mortal words. The implanted Word is effective in a believer's life because God is "watching over [His] word to perform it" and "every word of God proves true"[39] (Jeremiah 1:12; Proverbs 30:5).

Groups Large and Small

Paul's exhortation to "let the word of Christ dwell in you richly" (Colossians 3:16) was for the church at Colossae, and it continues to this day.

Some churches have committed to memorize Scripture together as a corporate body. But smaller groups can also benefit from memorizing verses together. Sunday school classrooms are ideal for learning new verses and reviewing old ones together. Children enjoy working together, playing games, and doing activities to help them remember a passage. Adults also benefit from the support of the group. Passages memorized for a class can serve for all of life. A teacher covering a chapter or book of the Bible over multiple weeks might choose

39. Adapted from Brian Eaton. "The Power of the Memorized Word in the Fight of Faith." Children Desiring God (Truth78) 2016 National Conference. Indianapolis, Indiana.

one or two verses that capture the theme of instruction. Not only does memorizing as a group encourage everyone to participate, but committing a thematic passage to memory will make it easier to recall, and apply the main point long after the class has ended.

A third possibility for memorizing in smaller groups within the church is the men's and women's ministries. Teaming up with brothers (men with men) and sisters (women with women) is a powerful way to apply God's Word to the unique challenges men and women face. There is a camaraderie and God-ordained structure to groups made up of one gender. Paul instructed Titus that older men are to teach younger men and older women, younger women. Seeing Scripture memory modeled by more mature believers, and hearing how it has served to help them grow in the Lord, serve others, and fight sin is a powerful incentive to imitate their way of life (Philippians 3:17).

Transformation, Not Speed

The main goal of a memory program isn't numbers or speed, but enjoying the blessing that comes with memorizing by feeding on God's Word day by day. Some people memorize quickly, others slowly. Some may focus on one or two verses at a time, others can retain chapters and even whole books of the Bible. The more an individual memorizes, the more he is able to memorize; practice improves a person's ability. Whatever the pace, each church member should ask God in prayer to sustain and bless his efforts to memorize and meditate on His Word.

The Power of Stories

It's helpful to hear fellow church members talk about how they've used memorized verses to minister to others. For example, an aspiring medical doctor carries the week's verse in his pocket to review during downtime and share it with his patients who show interest. "Blessed is the man who remains steadfast under trial, for when he has stood the test he will receive the crown of life, which God has promised to those who love him" (James 1:12).

Some have leaned on verses to persevere in their trials, or for comfort in sickness and serious injury. "For to me to live is Christ, and to die is gain" (Philippians 1:21).

Others have been helped by the memorized Word to not lose heart: A job-hunting college graduate responding to rejection letters with the hope of God's promises, "Be strong and courageous. Do not be frightened, and do not be dismayed, for the LORD your God is with you wherever you go" (Joshua 1:9). An overseas missionary dad rocking his collicky baby night after night, knowing he is memorizing the same verses as his friends at church back home, "For the eyes of the LORD run to and fro throughout the whole earth, to give strong support to those whose heart is blameless toward him" (2 Chronicles 16:9). A shared collection of testimonies can be a powerful encouragement for more members to join in memorizing.

Chapter 7
Fighting the Good Fight

Fight the good fight of the faith. Take hold of the eternal life to which you were called and about which you made the good confession in the presence of many witnesses.

—1 Timothy 6:12

If the life of faith is a good fight of faith, we and our children must be well-armed for this fight. Though the battle rages, many Christians are unskilled in using this weapon effectively. Committing the Word of God to memory makes this powerful weapon readily available and provides us with an ever-present counselor and protector from the enemy of our souls.

Fight Sin with the Word

Satan isn't our only enemy. Our own hearts draw us away from God and toward worldly pursuits. That enemy is not merely, or even primarily, outside of us. Hebrews 4:12 says, "For the word of God is living and active, sharper than any two-edged sword, piercing to the division of soul and of spirit, of joints and of marrow, and discerning the thoughts and intentions of the heart." We need that sword to do its work on our own hearts.

Theologian Albert Mohler says when we approach the Scriptures humbly rather than haughtily, "then it is not we who read Scripture, it is Scripture that reads us. Scripture untangles the human heart and unearths sin like no other book can." He says,

> Scripture is like a scalpel wielded by God to perform spiritual surgery. In conjunction with the Holy Spirit, the Word of God cuts through the sin and darkness of the human heart to restore spiritual health and vitality for Christ. Without the Word, we are as good as dead. God's Word, however, eradicates the disease of the human heart and breathes life where there is death.[40]

God's Word is key to our fight against indwelling sin and persevering in the faith.

Persevere in Faith with the Word

Jesus and His gospel are "the power of God for salvation to everyone who believes" (Romans 1:16)—not only the power for the initial faith of conversion, but the power for the everyday Christian walk of faith. This is why Paul, after instructing us to work out our salvation "with fear and trembling" said, "it is God who works in you, both to will and to work for his good pleasure" (Philippians 2:12, 13). God's work makes our work possible.

So, too, it's God's strength that makes us fit to fight. Before urging us to take up the armor of God for spiritual battle, Paul tells Christians to "be strong in the Lord and in the strength of his might" (Ephesians 6:10). Praise God that He is at work in us and for us so that we might say with Paul, "I have fought the good fight, I have finished the race, I have kept the faith" (2 Timothy 4:7).

In the Strength God Provides

We pray that God will equip every believer to take up this mighty weapon of the memorized Word. May He help us all, through His Word, to hold fast to His promises, to be killing sin, and to persevere in faith until the end.

> *For, "Yet a little while, and the coming one will come and will not delay; but my righteous one shall live by faith, and if he shrinks back, my soul has no pleasure in him." But we are not of those who shrink back and are destroyed, but of those who have faith and preserve their souls. (Hebrews 10:37-39)*

---

40. Albert Mohler, *Exalting Jesus in Hebrews.* (Holman Reference: Nashville, Tenn.), 61.

Lord Jesus Christ, the Incarnate Word of God, may You be pleased to cause Your words to abide in us, as we abide in You so that we might bear fruit that lasts, and might not sin against You. May our delight be in Your law; may it flood our thoughts day and night, filling us with truth and causing us to overflow with love. Make us strong in the faith through all of life's storms so that we will persevere to the end, as more than conquerors, by the word of our testimony. And all of this to the praise of Your glorious grace. Amen.

Appendix

Memorizing with Fighter Verses

Truth78 created the Fighter Verses to help believers fight the good fight of faith[41] (1 Timothy 6:12). Our collection of passages is called "Fighter Verses" because every believer is called to fight a spiritual battle. The offensive weapon God has given us is His Word (Ephesians 6:17).

The Fighter Verses have been uniquely selected for their effectiveness in arming Christians to fight the good fight of faith. These verses—52 passages per year for five years, 260 in all—focus on God's promises, His character and worth, killing sin, and hoping in God through the gospel. While every verse in the Bible is profitable (2 Timothy 3:16), these particular passages are "Fighter Verses" because they are especially useful in the fight *for* faith and *against* unbelief and sin. Memorizing them puts us at the ready in this battle.

In his sermon announcing the launch of the Fighter Verses church-wide memory program, John Piper explained the name:

> Jesus defeated the devil's temptations with the use of a memorized passage of Scripture. And in Ephesians 6:17, Paul called the word of God "the sword of the Spirit." We cannot successfully overcome sin and Satan without the present treasure of precious words of God—"fighter verses."[42]

Twenty-five years later, FighterVerses.com is still helping individuals, families, and church bodies memorize Scripture each week through a range of free tools and resources at FighterVerses.com.

Tools

- **FighterVerses.com**—Provides an overview of the Fighter Verses program and its application for individual, family, and church use; includes a weekly devotional blog, memory tools, and verse charts.

41. Originally, the Fighter Verses program was introduced by Children Desiring God, now Truth78.
42. John Piper, "Thy Word I Have Treasured in My Heart," January 5, 1997, desiringgod.org/messages/thy-word-i-have-treasured-in-my-heart

- **Bookmarks**—References and checkboxes help keep track of progress. Perfect for marking the location of a current memory verse in your Bible. Available in English, Spanish, French, and German.
- **Progress charts**—Printable memory charts for children to track their progress.

Resources

- **Fighter Verses App**—Portable encouragement with quizzes, songs, study, and review help. Includes additional Bible translations and multiple languages. Available from Apple, Google Play, and Amazon.
- **Songs**—Fighter Verses set to music to help people memorize quickly and easily at home or on the go.
- **Fighter Verses studies**—Provide deeper study of the weekly Fighter Verses passages. Ideal for family and classroom use. Leader guides, participant workbooks, journals, and coloring books for children available for Sets 1 and 2.
- **Journal**—Includes a year's worth of memory verses with room for notes and written prayers. Available for Sets 1 and 2.
- **Foundation Verses cards, visuals, and coloring book**—Seventy-six short passages, with full-color illustrations to help toddlers and pre-readers lay a firm biblical foundation for life.
- **Memory Cards**—For those who prefer to have the cards professionally printed on cardstock. A sturdy two-ring binder contains all five sets of Fighter Verses.
- **Extended Collection**—Companion five-year set, including Philippians and James, Romans 5-8, and the Sermon on the Mount, for those who want to memorize longer passages of Scripture.

Memorizing as a Church

Fighter Verses were debuted for church-wide memory in 1997. Since then we have found many ways to encourage Bible memory in churches:

- Seek pastoral support. When pastors and elders memorize Scripture, they provide valuable encouragement to the rest of their congregation.
- Recruit rotating volunteers to recite the weekly memory verse during the Sunday morning announcements.
- Ask your pastor to consider preaching about the importance of Bible memory at the start of each new year.
- Add testimonies and Bible memory strategies to your church blog or newsletter.
- Post the current Fighter Verse on your church website and social media feeds.
- Include the Fighter Verses in your welcome or events.
- Form a Bible memory team to brainstorm and implement strategies for encouraging the body to persevere in this challenging, but rewarding, discipline.

Small Groups

Sometimes it's more plausible to begin a memory program in church by starting with one or more small groups. Whether in the weekly home-gatherings, or in the men's and women's ministries, a regular gathering of several people is ideal for memorizing the Word together.

Sunday School

Children have an amazing ability to memorize Scripture, and what they hide in their hearts when they're young is likely to remain with them into adulthood. What a gift to give children verses to cling to as they grow and face trials and temptations. The Foundation Verses are ideal for pre-readers and include colorful visuals large enough to hang on classroom walls or whiteboards. The pictures prompt children's memories, helping them recall the verses they're memorizing each week.

Older children can learn longer passages using the Fighter Verses. This is especially fruitful when families work together on the verses during the week, then recite them in their respective Sunday school classrooms. Memorizing verses together is beneficial for all ages and stages of life. Some of the most dramatic stories of Bible memory have been from senior saints who started memorizing after retirement, and found themselves leaning heavily on God's promises as their health faltered.

Going Forward

Whether you memorize individually, with your family, or as a member of a church small group or congregation, we are eager to encourage you to take up the sword of the Spirit so that you can "be strong in the Lord and in the strength of his might" (Ephesians 6:10). It is our aim to help Christians "take up the whole armor of God, that [they] may be able to withstand in the evil day, and having done all, to stand firm" (Ephesians 6:13).

If we can be of service to you as you begin memorizing, please reach out to us at Truth78.org, or call (877) 400-1414.

Teaching the Word with Fighter Verses

Word-saturated conversations between parents and children are God's means for learning to fear, love, and obey God.

God told His people that His words were to be on their hearts so they could "teach them diligently" to their children, "talk[ing] of them when you sit in your house, and when you walk by the way, and when you lie down, and when you rise" (Deuteronomy 6:1-7).

How can parents know the Bible and talk about it with their children? It's not as easy as it once was before all the distractions and demands of our age. But it's still stimple: spend time together in the Word. Fighter Verses can help.

The short weekly passages are ideal for reading during mealtime. Parents can talk about the verse(s), ask questions to lead children to discover the meaning, and ask children to take turns bringing questions about the passage to the table. Drive time makes for captive audiences when we leave our devices unplugged. Use time in the car to practice saying the passage together or listen to the Fighter Verses songs to help you remember the words. Bedtime prayers are ideal for praying the promises of the Scriptures over children.

Making Bible reading and verse memorization part of your family's routine is key to doing it faithfully.

To make the most of the time you set aside:

Keep it short

A short instructional time that catches and holds a child's interest is better than a long drawn-out time that leaves the child bored and frustrated.

Keep it bite-sized

Keep instruction from being burdensome by teaching a word, phrase, or verse at a time, according to your child's age and attention span. The Bible is so rich that a single verse, or even phrase, can be plumbed for fruitful instruction.

Don't worry about being exhaustive. Instead, ask the Holy Spirit to guide you in teaching the points God puts on your heart. Better to spend several days on a small segment than try to cover everything in one sitting.

Keep it simple

It's fun to be creative with visuals and extras. But more isn't always better. Complex preparations often lead to days with little or no instruction because your schedule is packed. If you keep your Bible time simple, you'll be more likely to keep going consistently. Five to 15 minutes each day for a long time is far better than a one-time Pinterest-worthy production.

Simple lessons only require that you mull over the meaning of the verse, asking God how it applies in your child's and your life, and praying that God will make the verse alive in your hearts.

Define words

Look up any words your child doesn't know, and explain definitions in words he will understand.

Relate the unfamiliar to the familiar

Refer back to what your child already knows to help him understand a new concept. For example, when teaching Psalm 103:10, "he does not deal with us according to our sins," you might ask if he can think of a time in the Bible when God forgave someone who deserved punishment (e.g., Jonah's flight to Tarshish, David with Bathsheba, the Israelites' idolatry, etc.). Talk about how God was merciful, overlooking sin, possibly pointing to Micah 7:18 and Romans 3:25.

Use real-life situations to illustrate biblical truth

Use common experiences to help your child understand a biblical concept or the point of a passage. For example, the word *covenant* in Jeremiah 32:40 might be unfamiliar. *Agreement* is probably more familiar. You could use the example of agreeing on an allowance—the parents have an agreement with the child that they will give him a certain amount of money each month—to teach the concept of covenant.

Help your child interact with the truth of Scripture

Asking questions is the easiest way to encourage your child to interact with the text. For example, Psalm 34:9 says, "Oh, fear the LORD, you his saints, for those who fear him have no lack!" You could ask:

- What do you think this verse means?
- What other verse do you know that talks about the same thing?
- What does it mean to fear God?
- Can you think of a person you respect?
- Do you act differently around that person? How do you act differently?
- In what ways do you act differently to your little brother than you do to your teacher?
- What does this teach you about how we're supposed to act toward God?
- What does God promise to those who fear Him?

Lead your child to see how the Scripture applies to life

The aim of Bible instruction is not merely increasing knowledge, but also building faith. Help your child to see that God's Word relates to his own life by asking questions. Consider Psalm 56:3-4, "When I am afraid, I put my trust in you. In God, whose word I praise, in God I trust; I shall not be afraid. What can [man] do to me?" You might read the passage, then ask:

- Have you ever seen the truth of this verse in your life or in the life of another person?
- Do you have any fears?
- What are they?
- How will knowing this help you with fear?
- What can you do when you feel fear?
- What do you think God would want you to do now that you understand this verse?

Encourage your child to act on the Word of God

Ask the Holy Spirit to provide circumstances where your child can act on a newly discovered truth. And ask Him to bring that truth to your child's mind. Then encourage your child in his walk of faith.

Why Memorize Scripture?

By John Piper

First, a few testimonies: I have it third hand that Dr. Howard Hendricks of Dallas Seminary once made the statement (and I paraphrase) that if it were his decision, every student graduating from Dallas Theological Seminary would be required to learn one thousand verses word perfect before they graduated.

Dallas Willard, professor of Philosophy at the University of Southern California, wrote,

> Bible memorization is absolutely fundamental to spiritual formation. If I had to choose between all the disciplines of the spiritual life, I would choose Bible memorization, because it is a fundamental way of filling our minds with what it needs. This book of the law shall not depart out of your mouth. That's where you need it! How does it get in your mouth? Memorization.[43]

Chuck Swindoll wrote,

> I know of no other single practice in the Christian life more rewarding, practically speaking, than memorizing Scripture....No other single exercise pays greater spiritual dividends! Your prayer life will be strengthened. Your witnessing will be sharper and much more effective. Your attitudes and outlook will begin to change. Your mind will become alert and observant. Your confidence and assurance will be enhanced. Your faith will be solidified.[44]

One of the reasons Martin Luther came to his great discovery in the Bible of justification by faith alone was that in his early years in the Augustinian monastery he was influenced to love Scripture by Johann Staupitz. Luther devoured the Bible in a day when people earned doctorates in theology without even reading the Bible. Luther said that his fellow professor, Andreas Karlstadt, did not even own a Bible when he earned his doctor of theology degree, nor did he until

43. Dallas Willard, "Spiritual Formation in Christ for the Whole Life and Whole Person," *Vocatio*, Vol. 12, No. 2, Spring 2001, p. 7.
44. Charles R. Swindoll, *Growing Strong in the Seasons of Life*. (Grand Rapids, Mich.: Zondervan, 1994), 61.

many years later.[45] Luther knew so much of the Bible from memory that when the Lord opened his eyes to see the truth of justification in Romans 1:17, he said, "Thereupon I ran through the Scriptures from memory," in order to confirm what he had found.

So here are a few reasons why so many have viewed Scripture memorization as so essential to the Christian life:

1. Conformity to Christ

Paul wrote that "we all,...beholding the glory of the Lord, are being transformed into the same image from one degree of glory to another" (2 Corinthians 3:18). If we would be changed into Christlikeness, we must steadily see him. This happens in the word. "The Lord *revealed himself* to Samuel at Shiloh *by the word* of the Lord" (1 Samuel 3:21). Bible memorization has the effect of making our gaze on Jesus steadier and clearer.

2. Daily Triumph over Sin

"How can a young man keep his way pure? By guarding it according to your word....I have stored up your word in my heart, that I might not sin against you" (Psalm 119:9, 11). Paul said that we must "by the Spirit...put to death the [sinful] deeds of the body" (Romans 8:13). The one piece of armor used to kill is the "sword of the Spirit" which is the word of God (Ephesians 6:17). As sin lures the body into sinful action, we call to mind a Christ-revealing word of Scripture and slay the temptation with the superior worth and beauty of Christ over what sin offers.

3. Daily Triumph over Satan

When Jesus was tempted by Satan in the wilderness, he recited Scripture from memory and put Satan to flight (Matthew 4:1–11).

4. Comfort and Counsel for People You Love

The times when people need you to give them comfort and counsel do not always coincide with the times you have your Bible handy. Not only that, the very word of God spoken spontaneously from your heart

45. Richard Bucher, "Martin Luther's Love for the Bible," hopefaithprayer.com/scriptures/martin-luther-love-bible/

has unusual power. Proverbs 25:11 says, "A word fitly spoken is like apples of gold in a setting of silver." That is a beautiful way of saying, *When the heart full of God's love can draw on the mind full of God's Word, timely blessings flow from the mouth.*

5. Communicating the Gospel to Unbelievers

Opportunities to share the gospel come when we do not have the Bible in hand. Actual verses of the Bible have their own penetrating power. And when they come from our heart, as well as from the Book, the witness is given that they are precious enough to learn. We should all be able to sum up the gospel under four main headings: 1) God's holiness/law/glory, 2) man's sin/rebellion/disobedience, 3) Christ's death for sinners, 4) the free gift of life by faith. Learn a verse or two relating to each of these, and be ready in season and out of season to share them.

6. Communion with God in the Enjoyment of His Person and Ways

The way we commune with (that is, fellowship with) God is by meditating on his attributes and expressing to him our thanks and admiration and love, and seeking his help to live a life that reflects the value of these attributes. Therefore, storing texts in our minds about God helps us relate to him as he really is. For example, imagine being able to call this to mind through the day:

> *The Lord is merciful and gracious, slow to anger and abounding in steadfast love. He will not always chide, nor will he keep his anger forever. He does not deal with us according to our sins, nor repay us according to our iniquities. For as high as the heavens are above the earth, so great is his steadfast love toward those who fear him; as far as the east is from the west, so far does he remove our transgressions from us. As a father shows compassion to his children, so the Lord shows compassion to those who fear him. For he knows our frame; he remembers that we are dust. (Psalm 103:8–14)*

I used the word "enjoyment" intentionally when I said, "communion with God in the enjoyment of his person and ways." Most of us are emotionally crippled—all of us, really. We do not experience God in the fullness of our emotional potential.

How will that change? One way is to memorize the emotional expressions of the Bible and speak them to the Lord and to each other until they become part of who we are. For example, in Psalm 103:1, we say, "Bless the LORD, O my soul, and all that is within me, bless his holy name!" That is not a natural expression for many people. But if we memorize this and other emotional expressions from the Bible, and say them often, asking the Lord to make the emotion real in our hearts, we can actually grow into that emotion and expression. It will become part of who we are. We will be less emotionally crippled and more able to render proper praise and thanks to God.

There are other reasons for memorizing Scripture. I hope you find them in the actual practice.[46]

46. John Piper, "Why Memorize Scripture?" September 5, 2006, desiringgod.org/articles/why-memorize-scripture

Fighter Verses

By Topic

Anger
- Proverbs 16:32
- Proverbs 19:11
- Proverbs 29:1, 11
- Ephesians 4:26
- James 1:19-20

Anxiety
- Psalm 55:22
- Romans 8:31-32
- Philippians 4:6-7
- 1 Peter 5:6-8
- 1 John 4:4

Contentment
- Proverbs 22:1
- Philippians 4:11-13
- 1 Timothy 6:6-7
- Hebrews 13:5-6

Depending on Christ
- Matthew 11:28-30
- 2 Corinthians 12:9 [10]

Discipline
- Proverbs 3:11-12

Endurance
- 1 Corinthians 15:58
- Hebrews 12:1
- James 1:2-3
- James 1:4-5
- James 1:12

Eternity
- John 14:2-3
- 1 Corinthians 15:51-52
- Revelation 21:3
- Revelation 21:4
- Revelation 21:5-6 [7]

Faithfulness of God
- Deuteronomy 7:9
- Psalm 34:15-16
- Psalm 34:17-18
- Psalm 86:5-7
- Psalm 100:4-5
- Isaiah 46:3-4
- Philippians 4:19

Fear
- Joshua 1:9
- Psalm 27:1 [2-3]
- Psalm 56:3-4
- Psalm 118:5-8
- Isaiah 41:10
- Isaiah 43:1-3
- Matthew 10:28
- 2 Timothy 1:7

Forgiveness
- Isaiah 43:25

Generosity
- Proverbs 3:9-10
- Matthew 6:19-21
- Luke 12:32-34
- Acts 20:35
- 2 Corinthians 9:6-7
- 2 Corinthians 9:8

God's Goodness
- Psalm 34:6-8
- Psalm 84:10-11 [12]
- Psalm 103:1-4
- Psalm 103:5-7
- Psalm 103:8-10
- Psalm 103:11-14
- Psalm 103:15-16
- Psalm 103:17-19
- Jeremiah 32:40
- James 1:17

Gospel
- John 3:16-17
- Romans 1:16 [17]
- Romans 3:23-24
- Romans 5:8
- Romans 6:23
- Romans 10:13-14 [15]
- 1 Corinthians 15:1-3
- 2 Corinthians 5:21
- 1 Timothy 1:15
- 1 Peter 2:24
- 1 Peter 3:18

Guidance
- Psalm 23:1-2
- Psalm 23:3-4
- Psalm 32:8 [9]
- Psalm 37:23-24
- Psalm 86:11
- Psalm 139:23-24
- Proverbs 4:25-27

Humility of Christ
- Matthew 20:26-28
- 2 Corinthians 8:9
- Philippians 2:5-7
- Philippians 2:8-9

Joy
- Psalm 16:11
- Proverbs 17:9, 22

Life in Christ
- John 5:39-40
- John 6:35
- John 10:10
- John 11:25-26
- John 14:6
- John 15:5
- John 15:7
- Romans 12:9-10
- Romans 12:11-13
- Romans 12:14-16
- Romans 12:17-19
- Romans 12:20-21
- Romans 15:1-2
- 2 Corinthians 5:17
- Galatians 2:20
- Galatians 6:9-10
- Philippians 1:21
- Colossians 3:1-3
- 1 Thessalonians 5:14-17
- 1 Peter 2:9-10 [11]

Love
- Lamentations 3:21-23
- Lamentations 3:31-33
- 1 John 3:1 [2]

Loving God
- Deuteronomy 6:4-5
- Psalm 139:17-18
- Matthew 22:37-39

Obeying God
- Deuteronomy 10:12-13
- Proverbs 6:20-21
- Acts 5:29
- James 1:22-24
- James 4:7-8

Praise and Worship
- Psalm 34:1-3
- Psalm 96:1-3
- Psalm 96:6-8
- Psalm 96:9-10
- Psalm 100:1-3
- Psalm 103:20-22
- Revelation 5:12-13

Presence
- 2 Chronicles 16:9
- Psalm 23:5-6
- Psalm 139:1-3
- Psalm 139:6-8
- Psalm 139:9-10
- Psalm 139:11-12

Pride
- Proverbs 31:30
- Jeremiah 9:23-24
- Galatians 6:14
- James 4:13-14
- James 4:15-17

Provision
- Psalm 34:9-11
- Ephesians 3:20-21

Salvation
- Psalm 79:9
- John 1:12-13
- John 3:36
- Acts 4:11-12
- Romans 5:9-10
- Romans 8:29-30
- 1 Corinthians 1:18
- Ephesians 2:8-10
- Philippians 3:9
- 1 Peter 1:3-5

Sanctification
- Proverbs 4:23-24
- Matthew 5:3-6
- Matthew 5:7-10
- Romans 12:1-2
- 1 Corinthians 10:31
- 1 Corinthians 13:4-7
- Galatians 5:22-23
- Galatians 5:24-25
- Ephesians 4:31-32
- Philippians 2:12-13
- Philippians 4:8
- 1 Thessalonians 5:18-22

Security in God
- Psalm 91:1-2
- Psalm 91:3-4
- Psalm 91:5-6
- Psalm 91:7-8
- Psalm 91:9-10
- Psalm 91:11-13
- Psalm 91:14-16
- Psalm 121:1-2
- Psalm 121:3-4
- Psalm 121:5-6
- Psalm 121:7-8
- Proverbs 18:10
- John 10:27-30
- Romans 8:33-34
- Romans 8:35-37
- Romans 8:38-39
- Romans 14:7-8 [9]
- Philippians 1:6

Seeking God
- Psalm 9:9-10
- Psalm 27:4 [5]
- Psalm 34:4-5
- Jeremiah 29:11-14

Sin
- Proverbs 1:10
- 1 Corinthians 10:13
- Hebrews 3:12-13
- 1 John 1:8-9
- 1 John 2:15-17

Sovereignty of God
- Numbers 23:19
- Psalm 77:13-14
- Psalm 96:4-5
- Psalm 127:1
- Psalm 139:4-5
- Psalm 139:13-14
- Psalm 139:15-16
- Isaiah 40:28-29
- Isaiah 46:9-10 [11]
- Jeremiah 1:12
- Daniel 2:20-21
- Romans 8:28
- Romans 11:33-36

Speech
- Psalm 34:12-14
- Psalm 141:3-4
- Proverbs 15:1
- Proverbs 26:20
- Ephesians 4:29
- Colossians 4:6

Spiritual Warfare
- Ephesians 6:10-11
- Ephesians 6:12-13
- Ephesians 6:14-15
- Ephesians 6:16-17 [18]

Suffering
- Psalm 30:4-5
- Psalm 34:19-22
- Matthew 5:11-12
- 2 Corinthians 4:17-18
- Philippians 3:10-11
- 1 Peter 4:16
- 1 Peter 5:9-10 [11]
- Revelation 2:10

Supremacy of Jesus
- 1 Corinthians 2:1-2
- Philippians 2:10-11
- Philippians 3:7-8
- 1 Timothy 2:5
- Hebrews 1:1-2
- Hebrews 1:3-4

Trusting God
- Psalm 20:6-7 [8]
- Psalm 37:[1-2] 3-4
- Psalm 37:5-6 [7-8]
- Psalm 42:11
- Psalm 62:5-7 [8]
- Psalm 73:25-26
- Psalm 118:13-14
- Psalm 125:1-2
- Proverbs 3:5-6 [7]
- Isaiah 26:3-4
- Hebrews 11:6

Waiting on God
- Psalm 27:13-14
- Isaiah 40:30-31
- Isaiah 64:4
- Lamentations 3:24-26

Word of the Lord
- Deuteronomy 6:6-7
- Psalm 1:1-2
- Psalm 1:3-4
- Psalm 1:5-6
- Psalm 18:30-31

- Psalm 19:7-8
- Psalm 19:9-11
- Psalm 119:14-16
- Proverbs 6:22-23
- Isaiah 40:8
- John 8:31-32
- Romans 10:17
- Colossians 3:16-17

Work of Christ

- Isaiah 53:4-5
- Isaiah 53:6
- Matthew 9:13
- Luke 19:10
- Romans 5:18-19
- Romans 8:1
- Ephesians 2:1-3
- Ephesians 2:4-5
- Ephesians 2:6-7
- Titus 3:4-6
- Hebrews 12:2

Youth

- 1 Timothy 4:12

Fighter Verses in Bible Order

- Numbers 23:19
- Deuteronomy 6:4-5
- Deuteronomy 6:6-7
- Deuteronomy 7:9
- Deuteronomy 10:12-13
- Joshua 1:9
- 2 Chronicles 16:9
- Psalm 1:1-2
- Psalm 1:3-4
- Psalm 1:5-6
- Psalm 9:9-10
- Psalm 16:11
- Psalm 18:30-31
- Psalm 19:7-8
- Psalm 19:9-11
- Psalm 20:6-7 [8]
- Psalm 23:1-2
- Psalm 23:3-4
- Psalm 23:5-6
- Psalm 27:1 [2-3]
- Psalm 27:4 [5]
- Psalm 27:13-14
- Psalm 30:4-5
- Psalm 32:8 [9]
- Psalm 34:1-3
- Psalm 34:4-5
- Psalm 34:6-8
- Psalm 34:9-11
- Psalm 34:12-14
- Psalm 34:15-16
- Psalm 34:17-18
- Psalm 34:19-22
- Psalm 37:[1-2] 3-4
- Psalm 37:5-6 [7-8]
- Psalm 37:23-24
- Psalm 42:11
- Psalm 55:22
- Psalm 56:3-4
- Psalm 62:5-7 [8]
- Psalm 73:25-26
- Psalm 77:13-14
- Psalm 79:9
- Psalm 84:10-11 [12]
- Psalm 86:5-7
- Psalm 86:11
- Psalm 91:1-2
- Psalm 91:3-4
- Psalm 91:5-6
- Psalm 91:7-8
- Psalm 91:9-10
- Psalm 91:11-13
- Psalm 91:14-16
- Psalm 96:1-3
- Psalm 96:4-5
- Psalm 96:6-8
- Psalm 96:9-10
- Psalm 100:1-3
- Psalm 100:4-5
- Psalm 103:1-4
- Psalm 103:5-7
- Psalm 103:8-10
- Psalm 103:11-14
- Psalm 103:15-16
- Psalm 103:17-19
- Psalm 103:20-22
- Psalm 118:5-8
- Psalm 118:13-14
- Psalm 119:14-16
- Psalm 121:1-2
- Psalm 121:3-4
- Psalm 121:5-6
- Psalm 121:7-8
- Psalm 125:1-2
- Psalm 127:1
- Psalm 139:1-3
- Psalm 139:4-5
- Psalm 139:6-8
- Psalm 139:9-10
- Psalm 139:11-12
- Psalm 139:13-14
- Psalm 139:15-16
- Psalm 139:17-18
- Psalm 139:23-24
- Psalm 141:3-4
- Proverbs 1:10
- Proverbs 3:5-6 [7]
- Proverbs 3:9-10
- Proverbs 3:11-12
- Proverbs 4:23-24
- Proverbs 4:25-27
- Proverbs 6:20-21
- Proverbs 6:22-23
- Proverbs 15:1
- Proverbs 16:32
- Proverbs 17:9, 22
- Proverbs 18:10
- Proverbs 19:11
- Proverbs 22:1
- Proverbs 26:20
- Proverbs 29:1, 11
- Proverbs 31:30
- Isaiah 26:3-4
- Isaiah 40:8
- Isaiah 40:28-29
- Isaiah 40:30-31
- Isaiah 41:10
- Isaiah 43:1-3
- Isaiah 43:25
- Isaiah 46:3-4
- Isaiah 46:9-10 [11]
- Isaiah 53:4-5
- Isaiah 53:6
- Isaiah 64:4
- Jeremiah 1:12
- Jeremiah 9:23-24
- Jeremiah 29:11-14
- Jeremiah 32:40
- Lamentations 3:21-23
- Lamentations 3:24-26
- Lamentations 3:31-33
- Daniel 2:20-21
- Matthew 5:3-6
- Matthew 5:7-10
- Matthew 5:11-12
- Matthew 6:19-21
- Matthew 9:13
- Matthew 10:28
- Matthew 11:28-30
- Matthew 20:26-28

- Matthew 22:37-39
- Luke 12:32-34
- Luke 19:10
- John 1:12-13
- John 3:16-17
- John 3:36
- John 5:39-40
- John 6:35
- John 8:31-32
- John 10:10
- John 10:27-30
- John 11:25-26
- John 14:2-3
- John 14:6
- John 15:5
- John 15:7
- Acts 4:11-12
- Acts 5:29
- Acts 20:35
- Romans 1:16 [17]
- Romans 3:23-24
- Romans 5:8
- Romans 5:9-10
- Romans 5:18-19
- Romans 6:23
- Romans 8:1
- Romans 8:28
- Romans 8:29-30
- Romans 8:31-32
- Romans 8:33-34
- Romans 8:35-37
- Romans 8:38-39
- Romans 10:13-14 [15]
- Romans 10:17
- Romans 11:33-36
- Romans 12:1-2
- Romans 12:9-10
- Romans 12:11-13
- Romans 12:14-16
- Romans 12:17-19
- Romans 12:20-21
- Romans 14:7-8 [9]
- Romans 15:1-2
- 1 Corinthians 1:18
- 1 Corinthians 2:1-2
- 1 Corinthians 10:13
- 1 Corinthians 10:31
- 1 Corinthians 13:4-7
- 1 Corinthians 15:1-3
- 1 Corinthians 15:51-52
- 1 Corinthians 15:58
- 2 Corinthians 4:17-18
- 2 Corinthians 5:17
- 2 Corinthians 5:21
- 2 Corinthians 8:9
- 2 Corinthians 9:6-7
- 2 Corinthians 9:8
- 2 Corinthians 12:9 [10]
- Galatians 2:20
- Galatians 5:22-23
- Galatians 5:24-25
- Galatians 6:9-10
- Galatians 6:14
- Ephesians 2:1-3
- Ephesians 2:4-5
- Ephesians 2:6-7
- Ephesians 2:8-10
- Ephesians 3:20-21
- Ephesians 4:26
- Ephesians 4:29
- Ephesians 4:31-32
- Ephesians 6:10-11
- Ephesians 6:12-13
- Ephesians 6:14-15
- Ephesians 6:16-17 [18]
- Philippians 1:6
- Philippians 1:21
- Philippians 2:5-7
- Philippians 2:8-9
- Philippians 2:10-11
- Philippians 2:12-13
- Philippians 3:7-8
- Philippians 3:9
- Philippians 3:10-11
- Philippians 4:6-7
- Philippians 4:8
- Philippians 4:11-13
- Philippians 4:19
- Colossians 3:1-3
- Colossians 3:16-17
- Colossians 4:6
- 1 Thessalonians 5:14-17
- 1 Thessalonians 5:18-22
- 1 Timothy 1:15
- 1 Timothy 2:5
- 1 Timothy 4:12
- 1 Timothy 6:6-7
- 2 Timothy 1:7
- Titus 3:4-6
- Hebrews 1:1-2
- Hebrews 1:3-4
- Hebrews 3:12-13
- Hebrews 11:6
- Hebrews 12:1
- Hebrews 12:2
- Hebrews 13:5-6
- James 1:2-3
- James 1:4-5
- James 1:12
- James 1:17
- James 1:19-20
- James 1:22-24
- James 4:7-8
- James 4:13-14
- James 4:15-17
- 1 Peter 1:3-5
- 1 Peter 2:9-10 [11]
- 1 Peter 2:24
- 1 Peter 3:18
- 1 Peter 4:16
- 1 Peter 5:6-8
- 1 Peter 5:9-10 [11]
- 1 John 1:8-9
- 1 John 2:15-17
- 1 John 3:1 [2]
- 1 John 4:4
- Revelation 2:10
- Revelation 5:12-13
- Revelation 21:3
- Revelation 21:4
- Revelation 21:5-6 [7]

Truth:78

Truth78 is a vision-oriented ministry for the next generations—that they may know, honor, and treasure God, setting their hope in Christ alone, so that they will live as faithful disciples for the glory of God.

Our mission is to inspire and equip the church and the home for the comprehensive discipleship of the next generation.

We are committed to developing resources and training that are God-centered, Bible-saturated, gospel-focused, Christ-exalting, Spirit-dependent, doctrinally grounded, and discipleship-oriented.

Resources and Training Materials

Truth78 offers the following categories of resources and training materials to equip the body of Christ and Christian parents:

Curriculum

We publish materials designed for formal Bible instruction. The scope and sequence of these materials reflects our commitment to teach children and youth the whole counsel of God over the course of their education. Materials include curricula for Sunday School, Midweek Bible programs, Backyard Bible Clubs or Vacation Bible School, and Intergenerational studies. Most of these materials can easily be adapted for use in Christian schools and education in the home.

Vision-Casting and Training

We offer a wide variety of booklets, video and audio seminars, articles, and other practical training resources that highlight and further expound our vision, mission, and values, as well as our educational philosophy and methodology. Many of these resources are freely distributed through our website. These items serve to assist ministry leaders, volunteers, and parents in implementing our vision and mission in their churches and homes.

Parenting and Family Discipleship

We have produced various materials and training resources designed to help parents disciple their children. These include booklets, video presentations, family devotionals, children's books, articles, and other recommended resources. Our curricula include take-home pages to help parents apply what is taught in the classroom to their child's daily experience in order to nurture faith.

Bible Memory

Our Fighter Verses Bible memory program encourages and equips the church, families, and individuals in the spiritual discipline of Bible memory. The 260 Fighter Verses passages have been uniquely selected for their ability to arm Christians to fight the good fight of faith by focusing on God's promises, His character and worth, killing sin, and hoping in God through the gospel. The 76 shorter Foundation Verses help toddlers and pre-readers lay a firm biblical foundation for life.

For more information on any of these resources and training materials, please contact us.

Truth78.org • info@Truth78.org
(877) 400-1414